Pinocchio

Level 4

Retold by Nicole Taylor

Series Editors: Annie Hughes and Melanie Williams

Pearson Education Limited
Edinburgh Gate, Harlow
Essex CM20 2JE, England
and Associated Companies throughout the world.

ISBN 0582 428645

First published by Librairie du Liban Publishers, 1996
This adaptation first published 2000 under licence by
Penguin Books
© 2000 Penguin Books Ltd
Illustrations © 1996 Librairie du Liban

3 5 7 9 10 8 6 4 2

Design by Traffika Publishing/Wendi Watson
Illustrations by David Cuzik

All rights reserved; no part of this publication may be reproduced, stored in a retrieval system, or transmitted in any form or by any means, electronic, mechanical, photocopying, recording, or otherwise, without the prior written permission of the Publishers.

Printed in Scotland by Scotprint, Haddington

Published by Pearson Education Limited in association with Penguin Books Ltd, both companies being subsidiaries of Pearson Plc

---

For a complete list of the titles available in the Penguin Young Readers series please write to your local Pearson Education office or to:
Marketing Department, Penguin Longman Publishing,
80 Strand, London WC2R 0RL

Once upon a time, there was a carpenter called Geppetto. He lived in a small village. He was sad because he had no wife and no children. One day he decided to make a wooden puppet. He made two wooden arms and two wooden legs, two hands and two feet.

He made a wooden body and a wooden head, two eyes, two ears, and a nose. He was very pleased and named the puppet Pinocchio. He painted a big, happy mouth on Pinocchio's face, but as soon as he had finished it, the puppet jumped up and ran away.

Geppetto ran after Pinocchio, down the street and around the village, but Pinocchio ran too fast.

At last a policeman caught Pinocchio by the nose. Geppetto was very angry. A little girl said, "Geppetto is angry. I think he's going to kill the puppet. Put him in prison."

The policeman put Geppetto in prison. Pinocchio went back to Geppetto's house. He was so very hungry. He looked for some food. He looked in all the cupboards and boxes in the kitchen. At last, he found some food and ate it, then went to sleep next to the fire.

The next day, Geppetto came home. He was still angry with Pinocchio and banged on the door. But Pinocchio could not get up to open the door because the fire had burned his feet.
"I can't get up!" he cried. Geppetto had to climb in through the window.

When Geppetto saw Pinocchio with no feet, he felt very sad. "I'll make you some new feet," he said. "But you must promise to be a good boy and to go to school."

He made Pinocchio new wooden feet, and some beautiful paper clothes, and then sent him to school.

On his way to school, Pinocchio heard music. It came from a puppet show. He stopped to watch. The puppets called out to him, "You're a puppet, so come on up! Come on up to the stage with us." Pinocchio went into the puppet show. He was very good and everyone laughed and clapped.

After the show, the puppet master was angry. He was tall and ugly with a long, black beard down to the floor. He caught Pinocchio in his big hands and shouted, "I'll throw you on the fire."

Pinocchio and the other puppets were afraid.

Then the puppet master started to count the money from the show. There was a lot of money because people liked the show very much. The puppet master was happy and he gave Pinocchio a gold coin.

"Thank you, sir," said Pinocchio and quickly ran out the door.

Pinocchio decided to go home.

On the way, he met a cat and a fox.

"Why are you so happy?" they asked.

"Because I was in a puppet show today. The people liked it, and the puppet master gave me a gold coin. Geppetto will be very happy," said Pinocchio.

"A gold coin!" said the cat.

"Why don't you come with us?" said the fox. "We'll show you how to turn your gold coin into twenty gold coins. Then Geppetto will be very, very happy."

So Pinocchio went with the fox and the cat into a big, dark forest.

But the cat and the fox did not help Pinocchio. They jumped on him and tried to steal his coin. Pinocchio kicked and hit them with his wooden feet and hands. Then he ran away as quickly as he could.

He ran and ran through the dark forest trying not to fall over the trees.
The cat and fox ran after him and nearly caught him.
At last he came to a house and banged on the door.

It was opened by a beautiful blue lady.

Pinocchio told her about the gold coin, the fox, and the cat.

"Where's the coin?" asked the blue lady.

"I lost it," said Pinocchio, but as he was telling this lie, he had a strange sensation. His nose began to grow.

"No, no, I ...I hid the coin in the forest," said Pinocchio, but this was another lie. And his nose grew bigger and bigger each time he told a lie.

"Can you help me?" said Pinocchio. "My nose is getting bigger and bigger. Can you stop it?"

"That's what happens when you tell lies," said the blue lady, "However, I am the Blue Fairy, and I can make your nose small again."

The Blue Fairy called the woodpeckers who pecked and pecked Pinocchio's nose until it was small again.

Then the Fairy said, "If you promise to be good, Pinocchio, I will make you into a real boy. But you must go to school and work hard. You mustn't tell lies."

"I promise," said Pinocchio.

Pinocchio wanted to be a real boy. But he did not remember what he had promised. He saw a coach full of children pulled by donkeys. "Come with us. We're going to Playland. We just play and have fun all day!"

Pinocchio went with the children to Playland.

Playland was really fun! There was no work and no worries.

It was just fun. There were games.

The children played and played all day.

One day Pinocchio noticed a strange thing. The donkeys all had children's feet. Pinocchio was puzzled by this.

An owl was watching him.

"That's what happens to lazy children," it said. "They change into donkeys! If you stay in Playland all day and don't get on with schoolwork and don't help at home, you will change into a donkey too."

"Oh no! I don't want to become a donkey!" said Pinocchio.

Pinocchio decided to go home to Geppetto. He went by sea and swam and swam, but there was a big storm. The waves were very big. Suddenly, an enormous fish came out of the waves and opened its enormous mouth. Pinocchio saw its enormous teeth.

Pinocchio was inside the fish. It was dark and cold. Suddenly, he saw a light. It was a man with a candle. He went toward the man and could not believe his eyes. It was Geppetto.

"Geppetto!"

"Pinocchio!"

"I was looking for you when I fell into the sea and was eaten by this fish."

"I wanted to get home quickly and jumped into the sea," said Pinocchio.

"Let's try to get out of here."

They waited until the enormous fish was asleep and crept out of its enormous mouth and into the sea. They swam until they reached the sand.

They were exhausted, and Geppetto carried Pinocchio out of the water.

After they rested, they started to walk home. They walked through the forest and over the mountains until they reached their village. All the people were happy to see them back.

It made Geppetto and Pinocchio feel good.

Pinocchio told them all about the cat, Playland, and the Blue Fairy, and how his nose grew bigger when he told lies. He told some lies and showed them. When he told them about the enormous fish, they said, "No!"

"It's true!" said Pinocchio. "Look, my nose isn't growing!"

Geppetto and Pinocchio were home again. Pinocchio gave Geppetto the gold coin and said,

"I promise to be good from now on."

At that moment, Pinocchio changed into a real boy. He was real, just as the Blue Fairy had promised.

Geppetto was so very, very happy. He bought a beautiful new house and Pinocchio some real clothes. He made him a beautiful new bed.

From then on, Geppetto and Pinocchio lived happily ever after as father and son and Pinocchio never told any more lies.

Activities

Before you read

Read the sentence and choose the correct picture.

An enormous fish

An enormous nose

The man is happy

A wooden puppet

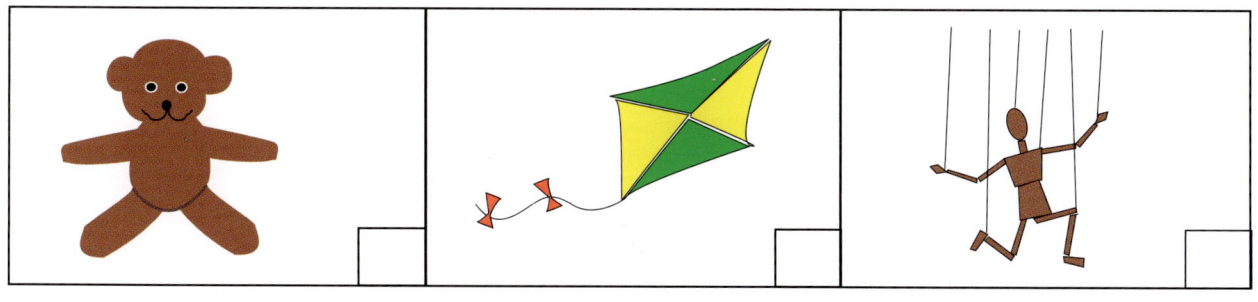

After you read

Look at the numbers and color the picture.

1. blue 2. yellow 3. red
4. pink 5. brown   6. green